3M's

The
Mims Morning
Meeting

SELLING TO INCREASE YOUR PROFITS

Special Thanks to

Vonda Hendricks

Chelbi A-J Mims

Donald Dean

Principals Component of Selling
Prescription Sales Training

Today tens of thousands of Americans are out of employment and are seeking a change in careers. Downsizing has pushed highly educated men and women to move from their chosen fields like accounting, primary and secondary education, legal, finance, contractors, health care and yes the broadcast media/communication. Many knowledgeable, highly motivated Americans are turning to a career in sales as a new occupation and innovative earnings. Why sales? A career in sale offers the greatest opportunity to achieve that six figure salary goal. A skilled trained sales professional can turn a six figure salary their first year on the job. Unfortunately, more than half of these new sales people will be fired or will quit 8 to

15 months into the job. Not, because they are not smart people nor because they are not stimulated but because they do not have the sales skills training and posses the cultural understanding needed to survive in a sales driven environment. The Mims Morning Meeting LLC has solved that predicament.

The Mims Morning Meeting is designed to increase the sales productivity of sales/marketing individuals/organizations. Created to refresh, train, retrain and introduce new sales method to business-to-business sales professionals in the 21st century. The Mims Morning Meeting breaks down each aspect of the formal selling skills process and accents the features and benefits of each; The Mims Morning Meeting bridges the gap left by most traditional sales training methods and techniques.   Today's companies don't train you on sales skills; they train you on product knowledge only.   The Mims Morning Meeting simplifies, clarifies, and identifies new avenues of sales techniques and explains them in its simple and easy to read booklet format. If you are new to the sport of selling or just need to sharpen up on a few skills and you need to do it quickly? The Mims Morning Meeting is for you! Remember all it takes to win in sell is that one differentiation that adds value to the prospects business.   The Mims Morning Meeting explains the working skills such as concentrative-listening, negotiations, today's probing, and many other topics and subjects. All designed to get you up to speed and keep you there. So, if you are new to the billion dollar world of selling or you are a season pro, 10 minutes a day with the Mims Morning Meeting will turn zeros into hundreds.

3M's

The

Mims Morning

Meeting

SELLING TO INCREASE YOUR PROFITS
Lesson 1

THE ART OF CONCENTRATIVE-LISTENING

THE ART OF CONCENTRATIVE-LISTENING

From the time we open our eyes in the morning until the time we close them at night, we are being sold something. A product or service is chasing us in some fashion. The average American, working an average day of ten hours with a 30- to 45-minute commutes, according to the web site infopleace.com will process over "100,000 bits of information in a single day". All the information is designed to be imaginative in nature and to get you, the consumer, to take action or buy into something. We are never removed from the grips of the advertisement. Everywhere we go— to church, the market, shopping mail, and on vacation-information to create a buying action is a culture of our environment.

Everyone in America is a salesperson. So why do you think your message is not being heard? In a world of instant internet, 24 hour television, all news all the time radio, e-mail on mobile phones and hundreds of wireless devices. How do you as the sales person complete with the thousands of propaganda sources? The answer is simple. You use these sources to help you get the ear and eye of those customers. In today's business first economy a new phrase has risen; du jour. Du Jour has to do with the proper type of information to be heard; by proper type information meaning first a clear and comprehensive understanding of the subject matter. That subject matter is not your environment, but that of the prospect environment- the prospects language, the culture, the business edict and purchasing index. If these are not terms you are familiar with you-don't be alarmed most sales people have not mastered these terms. Because they have not mastered these terms, they have longer sales cycles, lower Gross Profit Margins and work on accounts that do not fit their business models. The solution is simple answering the questions under the features section.

Features

THE ART OF CONCENTRATIVE-LISTENING

START WITH ANSWERING 10 FOUNDATIONAL QUESTIONS.

MEET THE PROSPECT. SOURCES FOR ANSWERS: INTERNET,
BUSINESS RADIO AND TELEVISION AND BUSINESS NEWSPAPERS.

1.What is the true business of a company and how long have they been a business?
2. How and why do they do what they do?
3. Who are their customers and why?
4. How does the company make a profit?

5. What immense changes does the company seek to make in the marketplace with the product or service they are offering?

6. What is the size and scope of the marketplaces of the company?

7. Who are the company's two direct competitors?

8. What is the difference between them and these two top competitors?

9. What is the financial environment of the company?

10. How did they grow the business year after year?

Benefits

THE ART OF CONCENTRATIVE-LISTENING

Answering these questions before you enter the first meeting with a new prospect will net great profits and rewards; today and in the future. The more elaborate your answers to these questions, the more detail your questions to the prospect will be, thus the preponderance of information will be obtained. "Go in smarter come out brilliant and engaged" are the goals of these questions. The benefits from adapting this method of selling are:

1.   Higher level of account penetration.
2.   Multiply departmental access.
3.   Shorter sales cycle.
4.   Larger Gross Profit Margin
5.   85% percent chance of future sales
6.   Accrued forecasting
7.   Opportunity to uncover two additional prospects
8.   Early determination of the true benefit of the prospect as they relate to your product/service.
9.   An outline of the future goals of the prospects.
10. Remove you from the role of a sales person in the eyes of the prospect and place you as a partner

status in solving this problem and future problems.

NOTES

The
Mims Morning
Meeting

SELLING TO INCREASE YOUR PROFITS
Lesson 2

THE ART OF REAL PROBLEM SOLVING

THE EYEOPENER®

THE ART OF REAL PROBLEMS SOLVING

Mr. And Ms. Sales Professional how does the Real-Problem in a company reveal itself? Every company has one or twenty-one Real problems that your product/service can solve. How do you locate that real-problem? This story may explain.

I have two of the greatest sisters-in-law any brother-in-law could want. The youngest, Linda, would literally, to use a cliché, give you the shirt off her back, then turn around and give you her bra. A kinder heart cannot be found. She has only one fault that is intolerable; she is the nosiest person I have ever had the privilege of meeting. She has to have all the information on everything and everybody she comes in contact with and the people they encountered. She knows the ins and outs of everyone and everything around her. Nothing is off limits; no conversation is taboo. Information to her is her lifeblood; she must have it in order to live. If it happens, Linda knows the details. She has the facts correct, down to the most meager detail on any topic. The television news, radio stations, newspapers and magazines of all types are her amalgamate. She thirsts for information about the things around her she has a true need for information. I have remarked that she has all the tools for a great sales person. She possesses a need for current information, the ability to find information and a systematic way to chronicle each and every fact for quick recall.

Features

ASTUE:of keen penetration or discernment. You must be mentally present for all accessible resources. Ears and eyes open at all times for the most smallest of details.

BELIEVABLE BENEFITS Real problems must be capable of eliciting trust. If the problem cannot be plausible and verifiable from at lease two credible sources, the information is deemed tainted and is of no benefit to you.

CLEAR: A clear and concise understanding of the real problem must be the cornerstone of the source. Information that is misinterpreted in any manner can lead to the wrong conclusion.

DISCREET If you discover a problem it belongs to you, not the problem but the discovery. You are under any obligation to reveal the contents to another. Wrong information in the wrong hands can hurt or kill the deal.

ELIMINATE Two questions should be asked. What advantage does this newly found problem give me over my competition? Can I annihilate my closest competitor with the information I now hold? If the answer is affirmative to both questions you have a real-problem.

Action to be taken

WHERE DO YOU FIND THE REAL PROBLEM?

Business operates for several reasons. All these reasons can be placed in one of two categories-to solve problems and to make money. In the quest for both there are real-problems that will arise. When that real-problem arises you the professional salesperson are there to uncover the solution. Here is how to find the real-problem in any company.

1. The morning newspaper is filled with business and the problems they face. (Wall Street Journal, The Washington Times, USA Today and LA Times)

2. Complying with new and old federal, state and local laws and ordinances is a large part of a business's real problems.

3. Rarely will one department in a business have a real-problem and it not effect another department or location.

4. Industry magazines are great barometers of business conditions and the problems they will face on account of changes and future events. (Oil & Gas Journal, Forbes,

Windows, Mortgage Banking and Business Finance)

5. Networking is a great way to find real-problems. To locate real problems requires in depth questions regarding the business environment and the changing conditions. Networking will only provide the who, you must determine the what, when and whereof the real-problem.

NOTES

_____

_____

_____

_____

_____

_____

_____

_____

_____

The

Mims Morning

Meeting

Lesson 3

The Art of Real-Change-Evolve

THE EYEOPENER®

THE ART OF REAL-CHANGE-EVOLVE

Change is the word used to describe the transition that occurs from same to different. This transition can affect a different thing in different ways. If you move a house plant from one location to another the plant may possibly receive plant shock. When seasons change from summer to fall many people will become ill with the flu. Moving ones place of residence is described as the most radical of changes in a person life and taking any medicine will change the chemical balance in the body and creat a negative reaction. Businesses will response in much the same manner. Negative reactions will occur when asked to change. When you ask your prospect to make a decision on your products or services you are

<u>creating change thus creating an environment for a negative reaction.</u>

Change is best served when it evolves in a progressive manner. That house plant if moved just moved a few feet per day to the other side of the room has no plant shock. Wrapping your body in fall clothing and covering your head will prevent illness and medicines in smaller douses allow the body to adjust thus no negative reaction to the change. The same rule applies in business-to-business selling. Walk, don't run is the process method. Allow the process to evolve and to advance at a pace agreed upon by you, and your prospect business.

Features

THE ART OF REAL-CHANGE-EVOLVE

<u>GRADUAL</u> Change must be accomplished by degrees. A step-

by-step process is the key to getting a prospect to agree to purchase your solution. Crawl, walk then run will guarantee a win every time. Start the change off slow and easy.

PROTECTIVE-Guarded is the watch word of the day when asking a prospect to make a decision. That change will affect the status of their job, effect how his/her peers view them in the future and that decision/change can affect the home life of the decision maker. As good as your solution is to you it may be the wrong thing to that decision maker. You must offer some protection with your solution. Protection to eliminate the risk and cover damage.

MEASURED- A tea spoon full or a shovel full which solution is best to solve the pending problem? Many times a tea spoon is easer to swallow than a shovel. It cost lest, it has less risk and it moves through the system with out interruption of day to day function. Don't use cannon to kill a fly.

COMFORTED– Ask anyone what they desire most in life and you will get a variety of answers. Every answer will lead back to one word comfort. They want a new car, more money larger home better spouses, smarter children or a beautiful garden. They want everything listed because they need to be comfortable. Have you made the prospect comfortable with your solution?

Actions to be Taken

THE ART OF REAL-CHANGE-EVOLVE

SEVEN STEP IN THE EVOLUTION

Step 1. Clearly understand the mission of the company's change.

Step 2. Locate where you are at this time and place within the company. Start, middle or end of the process.

Step 3. Outline where your prospect wants to go with this change.

Step 4. Outline names and titles of key personnel effected by the change and understand how change will affect them and their repartee.

Step 5. Now design a time line that ends on a date for change must accuse.

Step 6. Weekly validate your time line and make any adjustments needed and have them approved by the director of change/decision maker within the prospect company.

Step 7. Three weeks before the change must accrue take your

agreement in to the director of change/decision maker for review.

Notes

_____

_____

_____

_____

_____

_____

_____

_____

_____

The
Mims Morning
Meeting

Who is Your Prospect?

THE EYEOPENER®
Who is Your Prospect?

While looking for a new piano teacher for my fourteen year old daughter I telephoned and spoke to a Japanese gentleman that had come highly recommenced by a friend. My friend stated "he speaks English but you will never understand a word he says but he is a great piano instructor".

This got me thinking. Americans may all speak the English language but, we are not communicating with the same clear understanding. From industry to industry, company to company, from culture to culture the

English language is spoken in many dialects. Words spoken by one raised in the Japanese culture may be understood or interpreted quite differently than one raised in American culture. The words we hear, we use to convey our messages. These words are tools in our arsenal to influence and convert others as to the value of our products or services. No longer are our prospects all white American, all married and all male. The prospects for the 21st century are from Africa, Spain, Brazil, China, Russia and yes Iran. All here conducting business while using different English tongues.

Possessing the purchasing power of a large country. Having the capital to take your business to the next level and beyond. The use of the English language to convey the features of your product and services to develop applications for the solving of needs/problems is a key part of the sales process when addressing anyone where English is their second language.

Features

Who is Your Prospect?

SECOND LANGUAGE.

1. <u>Intense listening is required</u>. When communicating in English as a second language speaker, you must listen carefully and not wait to speak.

The more you listen the easier it is to understand. The ear becomes tuned to the speaker.

2. <u>Slow down you are in a school zone</u>. The pace of the process may be slower and cause extreme labor. Thus requiring added patience on your behalf. The pace will hasten with each meeting.

3. Understanding <u>cultural etiquette</u> can be helpful in nonverbal communications. The Internet and the Travel channels can be a warehouse of information when related comprehending the culture.

4. <u>Don't assume, ask</u>. Always ask the nationality of the person with whom you are speaking. One may looks like they are from Japan or China this may not be the case.

5. <u>Look but don't steer.</u> The clothing and adornments are a big part of the nonverbal communications. Understanding the meaning of the apparel is appreciated.

6. Religion symbols and alters to gods may adorn the business and touching such artificial may be considered offensive.

7. <u>If you don't understand ask</u>. Ask as many times as it take you to comprehend. You are there to help and build a sound working relationship. They will welcome your time and understanding.

Benefits

Who is Your Prospect?

Opening a new market for your products and services Larger gross profit margin per sale.

Less competition. Increase number of resells in future. Greater understanding of the business environment.

You become part of the solution team. Your personal brand is identified. You are empowered to move through the company to seek out others opportunities.

Your proposal will be viewed in a brighter light. New products and services will have a readily expected. You help author the handbook for projects in the future. Years of continued working relationships with valued customers.

NOTES

_____

_____

_____

_____

_____

_____

_____

_____

_____

_____

The Mims Morning Meeting

SELLING TO INCREASE YOUR PROFITS
Lesson 5

WHEN TO GET THE HELL OUT OF DODGE

WHEN TO GET THE HELL OUT OF DODGE

Sales professional waist time with prospects that are not going to buy.

If you have worked in the field of sales and sales marketing you have a story about the prospect that got away after you had forecasted it to close. Not only had you forecasted the closing for this month but, you purchased that new 50" television based on the commission you would receive.

How could I have mis-read this prospect, he told me I had the deal, why did they sign with my competition?

These are the questions you ask yourself on the first day of a new month after you missed your forecast. The other question is how

I explain this to the bosses, the ones at work and the one at home? To prevent this from occurring again read the prospect signs and signals, stop listening to the words coming out of their month. You have been reading signs all your life. When you were a child your parents gave you signs. You were aware when to ask for something and when not to ask by reading the signs and signals. When you drove into the office you read the signs in order to get to your destination safely. We are a world of signs and signals. Your prospect is no different they also give signs and signals each time you speak with them. You just have to learn the language. You must read the signs to determine the outcome of your work. The signs are clearly posted and easy to read.

Your prospect will use symbols to denote their actions.

You know them—not accepting your calls, and cancel appointments an hour before you were to a

Features

WHEN TO GET THE HELL OUT OF DODGE

1ST- Is the prospect involved in the sales/buying process?

A. Did the prospect <u>ask</u> for a demonstration of your product or service?

B. Will the prospect <u>pay</u> for a demo of the product or service?

C. Had the prospect given you <u>direction</u> on how to sell him/her?

D. Had the prospect gotten <u>other members</u> of his /her team involved with you in work with your solution?

E. Had he/she asked for <u>references or site tours or</u> others using your products or services?

F. Has the prospect called you with direct questions are you calling him/her to give information?

G. Can the person that said yes sign your agreement.

2nd⁻ Have you solved the real⁻problem the company is facing?

  H. What is the impact on the prospects bottom⁻line if he/she purchases your products or services?

  I. What is the return on the investment of this purchase?

J. What is the general rule for payback on investment set forth by the CFO of the prospect company.

K. Have you discussed what happens after the purchase is made?

L. Have you answered or reviewed the 14 questions in concentrative⁻listening?

Action to be taken

WHEN TO GET THE HELL OUT OF DODGE

1. When you can present your solution to the head not to the tail. (We all know what comes from a tail end)

2. Look for the real-problems to be solved not a symptom of the real-problem. (You don't place a Band-aid on a gun shot wound)

3. Close often.

4. Take others along to give you a reading on this prospect. (Before you married them you took them home to mother)

5. Ask other sales professional that have sold or lost deals to this prospect about their encounter.

(Today's environment requires a back-ground check)

6.   Do you understand how your solution will affect the prospect's business both domestically and internationally?
     (All medicines require instructions and will outline the effect on the total body)

7. Do your homework before you meet the prospect, during the process and just before the final close? (See booklet on Concentrative-listening)

8. If you want to know something read the sign; you can't go wrong.

Copyright ©

NOTES

OTHER LESSONS

3M's *THE MIMS MORNING MEETING*

Five Set Booklet Packages

Principals Component of Selling

Volume I

CONCENTRATIVE-LISTENING:
A quick study of developing great listening skills and the questions around them.

THE ART OF REAL PROBLEM
SOLVING: A quick study of finding the real trouble in a company and how to find it.

THE ART OF CHANGE
EVOLVE: A quick study of how businesses change.

WHO IS YOUR PROSPECT?:
How to locate that new and different prospect for selling.

WHEN TO GET OUT OF
DODGE PART I: A quick study in how to detect a proper buyer and not waste your time.

Volume II

CREATE A LIFE BRAND: A
quick study in becoming the brand you want to be.

EFFECTIVE PEOPLE: A quick study on Personal Development taken from the book "7 Habits of Highly Effective People by Stephen Covey

USING THE OUT METHOD TO SELL: A question booklet designed to help you think through the entire avenue in the sales process before the presentation.

THE BEST WAY TO GET ON YOUR FEET: A quick study way to jump starts your new sales occupation.

TOOLS OF A SALES PROFESSIONAL: A quick study of the tools needed to work in the sales profession.

Volume III

HOW TO BUILD A PROFITABLE PIPELINE: A quick study lesson on building a sales prospect base.

MOVING THE SALES PROCESS ALONE: A Different methods to speed up the sal.

THE ART OF SALES?: Is it an art or is it a sign?

THE ART OF WAR PART I: A quick study lesson into the book by the same name by Sun Tzu

THE 96 HOUR WEEKEND: A quick study into Time Management

Volume IV

IT'S THE ECONOMIC STUPID PART I: A quick study in understand and sourcing the economic.

THE GOOD, THE BAD AND THE UGLY: A quick study in account management and account support

A FEW DOLLARS-MORE: A quick study lesson in sales negotiating.

SELLING: A quick study lesson in Presentation Skills

CASUAL VS. BUSINESS DRESSING: A quick study in Dressing for Success in North America.

Volume V

THE GOVERNMENT OF SELLING PART I: A quick study into the politics of the sales office.

IT'S NOT WHAT YOU SAY: A quick study into the art of communicating

THE SITUATION ROOM: Cold Calling

DIRECTOR WITH E'S: Account Management

GET BUSY LIVING: The Closing

Volume VI

SELLING ABROAD: A quick study guide to selling internationally

NETWORKING PART I OF V: A quick study of face to face networking

KNOW THY SELF: A quick study into Prospecting

THE BEST WAY TO GET ON
YOUR FEET PART II: A quick study way to jump starts your new sales occupation.
PARADIGM & PRINCIPLES OF
SELLING: Selling

Volume VII
THE POSTMORTEM: The follow-up conversation after the… and what must be covered.
THE NETWORKING NEW
GAME: Social Networking
SELLING WITH A PARTNER: A quick study lesson in of partner selling
THE SEX OF ACCOUNT
MANAGEMENT: A quick study in the sexual characteristics of account management
TURNING SELLING INTO PLAY: How to have fun and sell too.

See our seven set book packs on Core Component of Selling, and the seven set book packs Progressive Component of Selling.

CONSULTING SERVICES ON
SKYPE VIDEO
fmims@mimsmorningmeeting.com

www.ingramcontent.com/pod-product-compliance
Lightning Source LLC
Chambersburg PA
CBHW040919180526
45159CB00002BA/540